Schizophrenia

A Guide to Understanding and Managing Schizophrenia

Table of Contents

Introduction

Society tends to initially misrepresent something and then run with it. The public begins to crave this dysfunction so strongly that there is simply no reason for the media to show the reality of the situation. The stimulation the false reality brings is, quite simply, more exciting. Although this concept can be applied to any multitude of societal issues, a particular one that keeps getting the shorter end of the stick is mental health. Humans lack the full capacity to identify with and understand things that are not physically obvious to us. Sure, our brains have a better process of conceptualization than most other living creatures, yet we continue to struggle to accept the validity of some of the most basic human struggles, such as mental illness.

The reality is that a reported 46.4% of the United States adult population experience mental illness at some point in their lives. Nearly half of American adults will deal with a mental or emotional disorder to some degree, yet far from all will be aware of this happening, let alone seek help in managing it. If this issue is such a commonly occurring one, why does society continue to stigmatize it? The truth is, although mental disorders have existed for the entirety of human history, their proper identification has not. Even with as much progress as we have made in properly diagnosing mental disorders over the past half-century or so, we still have a lot to learn about them.

Frighteningly, due to their existence not manifesting physically, their seriousness is often not equated with illnesses of the body. This not only leaves it stigmatized, but also under researched.

Schizophrenia is frequently presented as the scariest, rarest, most mysterious, and most dangerous mental disorder out there. You are definitely not the only person that has been told by society to think of schizophrenia this way, as this is what has been presented to the general public for decades and decades. It is not surprising, however, since our society is still struggling to fully grasp much more common disorders, such as anxiety disorders or depression.

A Beautiful Mind, an American film released in 2001, is one of the most popular movies centering around the topic of schizophrenia. It is based on the true story of a mathematician, John Nash, who developed schizophrenia in his 30's and later saw his disorder seemingly dissipate. On one hand, this movie serves the critical role of giving schizophrenia the exposure that is needed to eventually reach full societal acceptance and assimilation. It uses an effective plot line to show the progression of the character's disorder, including his eventual improvement in managing his symptoms. On the other hand, however, leaving this movie to act as the sole representation of schizophrenia can lead to further misunderstanding. With some scenes depicting dangerous scenarios posed to others by the main character's reaction to his hallucinations, one may be led to assume all individuals with schizophrenia pose a threat. This is not to say that the film should have cut out these scenes, but rather that the media is in dire need of more representation of schizophrenia in order to provide the public with an accurate perspective of the entire spectrum of the disorder.

For those that have never come into contact with schizophrenia themselves or through a loved one, its reality will likely remain mystifying and dark. It is only through proper education that we will ever be able to move past labeling the disorder of schizophrenia as something wildly bewildering and instead focusing on supporting and accepting those who suffer from it.

Looking for a Solution

There is quite a noticeable divide currently happening between the general population and specialists in the fields of psychology, biology, and psychiatry. With medical advancements virtually multiplying by the minute, science is making not just strides, but leaps in progress towards a better understanding of schizophrenia. The majority of the rest of the population, however, remains oblivious to most new discoveries or conducted studies. What they are being fed by the media tends to further increase their confusion or lack of knowledge. Schizophrenia does indeed have the potential of being a dangerous disorder, but not in the way most people think. Schizophrenia poses the biggest threat to the individual who lives with it - not others around them. The best way for schizophrenia to pose less of a danger to the individual is through increasing the general public's understanding of it.

By choosing to educate yourself on this topic, you have already taken the first step towards helping mend the damage done to individuals with schizophrenia. This will not only leave you more knowledgeable, but also well-prepared for any struggles that may come your way. Many resources on schizophrenia—and other mental disorders of similar severity—offer solely statistics or fact-heavy content that bombards the reader with information without offering any hope of resolution. This not only alienates those that are already overly scared of the disorder, but also repeats the same exact information that is offered by a majority of other, more easily accessible resources. Evidently, this can also cause further mental strain on those who are directly dealing with schizophrenia in their lives one way or another. To prevent this pointless rotation of identical information, it is important to provide resources that offer more than just the facts and stats. Instead, we should provide resources that teach about the entire spectrum of the disorder, past events that have contributed to our current understanding of it, and most importantly, how to prioritize individuals with schizophrenia over the disorder itself. That is exactly what this book aims to accomplish.

Chapter 1: Schizophrenia: An Overview

First and foremost, it is critical to understand that schizophrenia does not manifest the same way for all individuals and has a diverse range of effects. In fact, it is this uniqueness in each individual that makes schizophrenia so complex and has previously led so many specialists into confusion. Schizophrenia is defined as a chronic and serious mental disorder that can cause the affected individual to have a distorted perception of reality. It commonly affects the individual's thought processes as well as their ability to manage their emotions and behavior. The roots of the word come from the Greek words 'schizo' and 'phrene,' meaning 'split' and 'mind', respectively. However, this often leads it to be associated with dissociative identity disorder (DID), in which the individual possesses at least two distinctly different personalities. These are often confused, but they are two separate disorders with different symptoms and treatments. Schizophrenia is categorized as an incurable disorder and often requires treatment that lasts the entirety of a lifetime. The distortion of reality makes it incredibly difficult and often impossible for the individual to differentiate between what is real and what is a symptom of schizophrenia. It can cause the individual to feel as if they have lost touch with reality, making everyday tasks and undertakings incredibly difficult. No doubt, schizophrenia is quite a challenging disorder to live with.

Currently, it is calculated that schizophrenia affects 1.2% of the American population. At first glance, that 1.2% may not sound like much, however, that still leaves as many as 3.2 million people in the United States living with the difficulties that come with this disorder. Although it is technically incurable, the treatments offered professionally are highly effective and can help many individuals with the condition lead normal lives. Shockingly, per year, approximately 40% of people with schizophrenia do not receive treatment. Leaving schizophrenia untreated or even undertreated puts the person at risk of developing worse symptoms and increases their chances of coming across future complications.

Schizophrenia often comes along with, or causes, other mental illnesses or comorbidities. One of the most common issues it leads to is the development of a social anxiety disorder. This often stems from the fact that many people with schizophrenia become increasingly less social and withdraw from many social interactions. With time, many find themselves unusually anxious when put in certain social situations. In addition to anxiety, depression can develop alongside schizophrenia. In fact, one in four people diagnosed with schizophrenia also meet the criteria for a diagnosis of depression. Often, a lack of adequate treatment is to blame for this. Something this combination is often confused with is schizoaffective disorder. Unlike schizophrenia, which is often the cause of an individual's depression, people diagnosed with schizoaffective disorder exhibit symptoms of both schizophrenia and a severe mood disorder, such as major depressive episodes or bipolar disorder, simultaneously. Schizoaffective disorder is diagnosed even more rarely, with an estimate that only 0.3% of people will develop it over the course of their life.

Unfortunately, due to the common complications of various anxiety disorders and depression caused by it, people living with schizophrenia are significantly more likely to experience suicidal thoughts. In fact, studies have shown that the suicide rate for people with schizophrenia is more than 20 times higher than for people without the disorder. Contrary to what many people may believe, it is generally not schizophrenia-based symptoms that push people towards suicidal thoughts. More commonly, it is the feelings of hopelessness, isolation, worthlessness, and realization of the negative effects of schizophrenia that are largely responsible for this phenomenon.

People with schizophrenia can face lots of discrimination, often fatally. In the healthcare system, many people with schizophrenia are overlooked. In other words, many of their physical health issues go untreated due to medical professionals falsely assuming that the symptoms they claim to have, are not real. Because of these kinds of issues, the life expectancy for a person with schizophrenia is up to 20 years less than the average life expectancy for a person living without a major mental disorder. Even after accounting for the higher rate of suicide prevalent in people with schizophrenia, their mortality rate remains substantially higher than expected. Diseases—namely, cardiovascular, metabolic, and infectious—are the leading physical illnesses that go undertreated and contribute to these statistics of premature death. Substance abuse is also considerably higher in people with schizophrenia. Most often, substance abuse begins out of the individual's attempt to relieve their symptoms, numb feelings of associated depression, and cope with the difficulties of dealing with stigma. The medical system's failure to accommodate and treat people with schizophrenia on equal terms leaves many at risk.

Onset and Causes of Schizophrenia

Schizophrenia is most often developed when people are in their 20's to mid-30's, with men commonly developing symptoms earlier than women. Some have theorized that women's estrogen production during puberty may be responsible for protecting them against the onset of schizophrenia for longer. It is extremely rare for a person to be diagnosed with schizophrenia earlier than 12 years of age. Other than its natural tendency to develop in early adulthood, it is also incredibly hard for some parents to be able to distinguish their child's normal behaviors from warning signs of schizophrenia. Many parents are led to think that the child is simply developing at a somewhat slower rate or that their immaturity is to blame.

The causes of schizophrenia are still being researched, with no fully conclusive results yet found. So far, the disorder's development is believed to be caused by a combination of factors, including:

- Genetics
- Mother's pregnancy or birth complications
- Environmental factors
- Structural and physical changes in the brain
- Hormonal changes
- Brain injury

Genetically speaking, no singular gene has so far been found to be responsible for the onset of the condition. However, a genetic link is often present. Studies have shown that, for people with an identical twin suffering from schizophrenia, their chances of developing the disorder themselves are up to 65%, compared to the 1% chance shared by the general population. For biological children of parents who are both diagnosed with the disorder, the chances are 50%. Although there is a multitude of evidence supporting the existence of a genetic connection, the exact inheritance pattern remains unclear. Sometimes, genetic mutations are at play. A minor change within genes—as seemingly insignificant as a deletion or duplication of a single nucleotide—may automatically cause the individual to be at a higher risk of developing the condition.

Many professionals believe that individuals with schizophrenia are more likely to have experienced some form of complications during their mother's pregnancy or birth. Specific aspects that could potentially cause the development of schizophrenia include:

- Lower than average birth weight
- Premature birth
- Birth asphyxia

Other than those three, it is theorized that the health of the mother during pregnancy could also have an effect—specifically, if she had endured a virus. The commonly proposed explanation is that these factors may influence the brain development in the fetus.

Factors such as gene mutations, inheritance, and birth complications that are completely out of the individual's control do not mean that they will definitely develop schizophrenia. In fact, certain environmental factors arguably play a much larger role in determining whether or not an individual will develop the condition. Childhood trauma is one of the most common triggers of schizophrenia, with kids who experience severe cases of it being three times more likely to have schizophrenia when they are older. Furthermore, patients with a psychotic disorder who were exposed to trauma in their childhood were two times more likely to act violently than those who were not exposed to trauma. This causes many to believe that the experiences a child goes through as they develop is one of the most influential pieces in the development and severity of schizophrenia later in life. As many as 85% of patients with schizophrenia report some type of childhood trauma or abuse.

It has long been reported that men were more likely to develop the condition earlier than women, and with stronger severity of symptoms, on average. This difference puzzled scientists for a long time, but recent studies have supported the hypothesis that estrogen acts as a buffer for the onset of the condition. In fact, out of 276 women with schizophrenia that were admitted to a psychiatric care center, 127 were admitted at a point in their hormonal cycle in which there was less estrogen present in their system. With estrogen most likely playing a crucial role in schizophrenia, it is no surprise that men fall victim to it earlier and more harshly.

One influence that is currently being explored in relation to schizophrenia is the use of drugs in adolescence and early adulthood. When people partake in drugs, such as cocaine, LSD, cannabis, or amphetamines, they often experience psychotic symptoms for the duration of their high. Although drugs themselves do not directly cause schizophrenia, high usage of cannabis in teen years increases the individual's chances of developing it. Many people who unknowingly carry certain brain chemistry-altering genes and use cannabis regularly are putting themselves at higher risk. People who start using cannabis earlier further increase this risk, as their brain is right in the midst of its development and its changes are highly vulnerable to being influenced.

Differences in Brain Structure and Function

Many of the factors discussed above were all examples of things that could influence a change in the structure, function, or chemistry of the brain. Some are even calling to categorize schizophrenia specifically as a brain disease. The majority of these physical changes within the brain can actually be observed through computed tomography (CT) and magnetic resonance imaging (MRI). Often, a person with schizophrenia will be put through these scans following their first psychotic episode. Through these techniques, the presence of enlarged ventricles and cortical atrophy are commonly seen in patients with schizophrenia. In other words, the brains of people with schizophrenia have enlarged cavities that transport cerebrospinal fluid, along with a process in which the outer part of the brain progressively degenerates. The longer a person has dealt with schizophrenia, the more enlarged their ventricles become. This is evidence that schizophrenia causes very calculable physical brain health differences and not just psychological symptoms.

Grey matter in the brain is another big concern for people with the condition. It is arguably one of the most important structures within the brain, responsible for allowing the brain to adequately process information. Its grey color comes from its high concentration of neuronal cell bodies and glial cells. In patients with schizophrenia, the volume of grey matter is reduced by an average of 25%. In fact, the higher the severity of the patient's symptoms, the less grey matter they have. A reduced amount of this grey matter is commonly associated with Alzheimer's disease, depression, and post-traumatic stress disorder (PTSD). This could explain why so many people with schizophrenia are considerably more prone to developing depression. In less extreme cases, less grey matter is associated with a decrease in cognitive functions, such as learning ability and quality of memory.

The very prevalent experience of childhood trauma among people with schizophrenia also plays a big role in identifying factors that may trigger the development of the condition. Specifically, it has been found that the brain's connectivity between its posterior cingulate—a structure that affects visual attention and executive motor function—and the amygdala—responsible for our ability to process strong emotions, such as fear and pleasure—is significantly decreased. Not only does this worsen the person's cognitive abilities, but it consequently sets them up to be more likely to develop schizophrenia.

Dopamine Hypothesis

The dopamine hypothesis was first proposed when it was discovered that dopamine is a type of neurotransmitter in the brain. A neurotransmitter is basically a chemical messenger from neurons to other neurons, muscles, or glands. These neurotransmitters are responsible for regulating certain processes, such as:

- Heart rate
- Breathing functions
- Digestion
- Sleep
- Mood
- Appetite
- Concentration
- Muscle movement

The neurotransmitter dopamine is specifically responsible for our ability to feel pleasure. It also plays a role in our focus and motivation levels. There are two specific dopamine neurotransmission receptors whose activities may influence the strength of certain schizophrenic symptoms, called D1 and D2. The former is responsible for details like memory, attention, and impulse control, while the latter is focused on factors like sleep, attention, memory, and learning.

The dopamine hypothesis suggests that the activity levels at which these two dopamine neurotransmission receptors function, influences the symptoms of schizophrenia. Particularly, it is theorized that if the D2 receptors are hyperactive and increase their transmission of dopamine, the positive symptoms of schizophrenia are stronger. On the flip side, the negative and cognitive symptoms are attributed to the hypoactivity of the D1 receptors.

This hypothesis plays a critical role in supporting the connection between childhood trauma and the development of schizophrenia. The stress sensitization theory states that children who had a rougher environment growing up are more prone to developing mental illnesses. In the scope of schizophrenia, this is applicable in that stress sensitization increases the reactivity of a person's hypothalamus-pituitary-adrenal axis (HPA), which is responsible for providing appropriate reactions to stress. When the HPA's reactivity is increased, it causes the overstimulation of the previously discussed D2 receptors and increases the presence of positive schizophrenic symptoms.

Chapter 2: Signs and Symptoms

Schizophrenia, as mentioned before, has an extremely varying set of symptoms. It is critical to look out for your own or your loved one's signs of schizophrenia, as treatment for it should be sought out as early as possible. Waiting to get help for schizophrenia means the grey matter and overall brain volume continue to decrease and can cause serious complications that are much more difficult to treat later on.

What is seen in the media is not accurately representative of what schizophrenia most commonly looks like. When the media does focus on real-life cases, it usually only focuses on the most severe incidents of schizophrenia, creating the illusion that all cases are like that. This could not be further from the truth, which involves a spectrum of symptoms that affect different cognitive abilities, sensory issues, and behaviors. A person could exhibit only some of the symptoms and not others, while another person's symptoms may change altogether over the course of the condition. Interestingly, a person who experiences a later onset of schizophrenia is more likely to see a gradual decrease in associated symptoms.

Schizophrenia is generally a quite debilitating disease, with difficulties of understanding stimuli and choosing an appropriate response being some of the leading indicators of the condition. An example of this would be smiling or laughing after receiving news of a loved one being hurt or passing away. For the individual affected by schizophrenia, this often causes them to feel out of touch or confused by reality. This inability to properly sort through events and provide a fitting response is a sign of what is often called the 'inappropriate affect.' The inappropriate affect is often a sign of other psychotic disorders, such as schizophrenia, but it can be a standalone disorder as well. It can be recognized by a severe reduction in a person's emotional expression. To an outsider, the inappropriate affect appears to manifest in people with schizophrenia through strange reactions due to their hallucinations or paranoia about other people's actions.

Phases of Schizophrenia

There are three distinct phases of schizophrenia that occur differently in each affected individual. These three include:

1. The prodromal stage
2. The active stage
3. The residual stage

The Prodromal Stage

The prodromal stage is the earliest stage of the condition, during which the individual undergoes subtle changes in their cognition and behavior. The symptoms of this prodromal stage are not generally associated with what most people think of when they think about schizophrenia. This leaves most people not at all aware of the fact that they are actually going through early stages of the condition. Symptoms during the prodromal stage include:

- Mood swings
- Difficulty concentrating
- Abnormal sleep patterns
- A new appearance of depression or anxiety
- A sense of mistrust in others that previously did not exist
- Social withdrawal
- Lack of energy and motivation
- Loss of interest in things that used to bring pleasure

The prodromal stage of the condition can last as little as several weeks to as long as several years. Approximately 75% of people with schizophrenia report having gone through the prodromal stage. Detecting schizophrenia within this early stage can greatly benefit the individual, as treatment during this stage can potentially prevent symptoms of psychosis that would appear later. Unfortunately, treatment is extremely rare at this stage, as many people exhibiting the symptoms common to the prodromal stage of schizophrenia are showing signs also seen in other mental illnesses; differentiating who will and who will not go on to develop the later stages of schizophrenia is incredibly difficult. Furthermore, most outsiders who observe a loved one exhibiting these symptoms will not think it is a sign of schizophrenia and assume it is a temporary behavioral phase. It does happen, however, that some people in the prodromal stage of schizophrenia never advance past it.

The Active Stage

The next stage of schizophrenia is the active stage, also known as acute schizophrenia; it includes the most obvious and characteristic signs of the condition. On average, a person who is at this stage of the condition has already been showing signs of it for two years leading up to this point. During the active stage, medical professionals used to classify the condition into one of the following five subtypes:

- **Catatonic schizophrenia.** This is a type of schizophrenia in which the affected individual has periods of time during which they move very little and do not respond to requests. This can be offset by other periods of time filled with hyperactivity and mimicking of others' movements or speech.

- **Disorganized schizophrenia.** In this form of schizophrenia, the person severely struggles to maintain concentration. They are likely to switch to topics of no connection and often say illogical things.

- **Paranoid schizophrenia.** Individuals with paranoid schizophrenia experience many delusional thoughts and struggle to differentiate them from regular thinking. Some believe the media they observe is sending them specific messages while others are convinced of others' malintent.

- **Residual schizophrenia.** Similar to the third stage of schizophrenia, the residual type used to be assigned to those individuals who had a history of schizophrenic episodes but no longer exhibited them.

- **Undifferentiated schizophrenia.** This subtype used to be assigned to individuals who exhibited some symptoms of schizophrenia but not enough to be considered suffering from one of the above categories.

However, this system did not work well for diagnosing the condition due to many overlaps between the proposed subtypes. For this reason, medical professionals no longer try to categorize each individual's unique form of schizophrenia into categories and instead examine it as a spectrum of types and intensities of symptoms.

Positive, Negative, and Cognitive Symptoms

Over the course of schizophrenia, most people develop a combination of three types of symptoms. The peak of these symptoms occurs during the active phase, with positive symptoms sometimes decreasing in the residual phase. The three types include:

- Positive symptoms
- Negative symptoms
- Cognitive symptoms

Positive symptoms are named after those that provide the presence of symptoms or an exaggeration of normal functioning. They tend to cause the individual to feel out of touch with reality and severely affect the person's thought processes, perceptions, and behaviors. Positive symptoms can include:

- **Hallucinations.** A person perceives the surrounding world differently than others do. Hallucinations can affect all five senses: hearing, sight, touch, and even the senses of smell and taste. Often, people with schizophrenia who suffer from hallucinations will hear things that others do not, feel things on their body, such as something touching them, or see visions of nonexistent light, deformations, and even realistic-looking people. The most common hallucinations amongst people with schizophrenia are auditory and visual, with the other three being reported much less frequently.

- **Delusions.** The affected individual is convinced of beliefs that are not true. Most often, these ideas seem strange to the outside person. In fact, there are six main types of delusions common to schizophrenia:

- ○ **Persecutory delusions** are when the person believes someone is out to 'get them.' They may think someone is tracking, tricking, stalking, or hunting them down.

- ○ **Referential delusions** cause people to think that public media contains secret messages that are specifically intended for them.

- ○ **Somatic delusions** convince the person that there is something deeply wrong with their body. This conviction could be one of realistic health problems or one of nonexistent health issues, such as being infested by insects.

- ○ **Erotomanic delusions** include irrational beliefs tied to one's romantic relationships. For example, they could be convinced that a celebrity is in love with them.

- ○ **Religious delusions** are centered around religious beliefs and figures. The individual may believe they are a deity of sorts or that they are possessed by a demon.

- ○ **Grandiose delusions** occur when a person is convinced that they are some type of famous public figure.

- **Disorganized thoughts.** The person is unable to form logical thoughts or express what is on their mind. Often, this manifests as quick shifts in topics, confusing combinations of words, and more.

- **Abnormal movement.** A person with schizophrenia can exhibit strange movements and motor functions. This is often associated with catatonic behavior.

The first two of these positive symptoms, hallucinations and delusions, are both psychosis symptoms. They cause a detachment from the reality of life and make it hard for some people to identify if what they are experiencing is real or fake. Eventually, with enough proper care, the person can learn to distinguish between the two and adapt to living in reality.

Unlike positive symptoms, negative symptoms are named after the fact that they take away some characteristic of the person's normal mental function. Primary negative symptoms are often regarded as the underlying symptoms of schizophrenia that are there whether or not the positive symptoms are. Secondary negative symptoms can also include those that are caused by the medication used to treat schizophrenia itself. In fact, many people who age and experience a decrease in positive symptoms will also see an increase in the severity of negative symptoms. These symptoms affect both the inner world of the person as well as how they express themselves, which includes:

- A lack of interest
- Social withdrawal
- A lack of pleasure
- Not being able to keep up with daily life requirements, such as hygiene
- A lack of emotional expression
- Emotionless voice when speaking
- A lack of eye contact

Scans such as the MRI or the Positron Emission Tomography (PET) have shown that the activity levels in the middle frontal cortex and inferior parietal cortex of the brain for patients of schizophrenia are significantly lower than those of the general population. Furthermore, scientists have found that the less activity there is in these areas, the stronger the person experiences negative symptoms.

Paul Eugen Bleuler, a Swiss psychiatrist of the 19th and 20th centuries, grouped the negative symptoms into what are now known as the four A's:

- Alogia: a person's extreme lack of speech
- Autism: the person's disconnection from external reality
- Ambivalence: the extreme reactions exhibited by a person with schizophrenia
- Affect blunting: certain symptoms of the individual's being masked until triggered by an outside event

The four A's are believed to be symptoms of schizophrenia that are present for the entirety of its duration. It is these fundamental symptoms proposed by Bleuler that have helped modern scientists expand on the presence of negative symptoms in patients of schizophrenia.

The last modern category of schizophrenic symptoms is cognitive, meaning they slow down the brain's ability to process information. These affect a person's thinking, memory, and planning capabilities. Sometimes, cognitive symptoms are quite subtle, while for others, they are severe and persistent. Cognitive symptoms include:

- Trouble concentrating
- Trouble absorbing new information
- Difficulty expressing their ideas

In accordance with the previously examined connection between childhood trauma survivors and schizophrenia, the type of experiences the patient went through as a child may influence which symptoms they suffer from. For example, studies show that children who experienced sexual abuse are more likely to develop hallucinations, and children who grew up in a children's home are more likely to develop paranoia. This further supports the idea that the experiences lived as a child affect brain function in such a way that makes the onset of schizophrenia and its symptoms considerably more likely.

The Residual Stage

The last stage of schizophrenia is the residual stage. This can be thought of as a stage of gradual recovery—at least a decrease—in certain symptoms. More often than not, individuals in the residual stage do not experience severe symptoms, such as hallucinations or delusions. The symptoms common to this stage match up with the negative symptoms of the condition. Unfortunately, depression is quite common to those in the residual phase, as they recognize the effects that schizophrenia has had on them and their life. By properly monitoring any worsening symptoms of depression or relapses of schizophrenic episodes, the person is more likely to maintain stable emotional wellbeing. In order for a person to safely progress to this stage, proper measures must be taken during the active stage in terms of treatment. Otherwise, left untreated, the symptoms of the active stage can remain for months at a time and reoccur quite often. This poses a great threat to the person's own health as well as decreases their chances at leading a regular life in society.

Common Experiences

Triggers are highly stressful events whose occurrence may cause the onset of schizophrenia for people who are at risk of developing it. The most commonly reported triggers are:

- Death of a loved one
- Job loss
- Homelessness
- The end of a relationship, including divorce
- Abuse: physical, sexual, or emotional

These and other events may cause the individual to experience a severe shock or amount of stress that causes the brain to start functioning abnormally.

Some specialists actually divide phases of schizophrenia even further, beyond just the prodromal, active, and residual stages. In particular, they examine the prodromal stage as two parts: the initial prodromal stage, in which symptoms are extremely mild, and the advanced prodromal phase, where subclinical symptoms strengthen. The active stage is then divided into two as well, with the early psychosis phase, where symptoms manifest as psychotic episodes at their worst, and the middle phase, where symptoms are still active but not as common. In this method of categorization, the residual stage is called the 'late illness phase,' but its symptoms remain the same as in the three-category system.

An interesting connection that has been observed over the course of the existence of recognized schizophrenia is one with religion and spirituality. As seen with positive symptoms, many religious aspects are often tied to people's experiences of schizophrenia. There are numerous similarities that overlap between auditory and visual hallucinations and religious experiences. In fact, many people tend to go to a priest for help rather than a medical professional when first coming into contact with schizophrenic delusions and hallucinations. Many delusions and hallucinations are directly parallel to experiences of those who seek exorcisms: demonic apparitions, demonic deformities of their own bodies, being possessed by a demon, etc. For example, Christian and Roman Catholic patients with schizophrenia are more likely to have religious delusions of guilt and sin than patients who believe in other religions. Although no conclusions have yet been made in terms of the relationship between schizophrenia and religiousness, this goes to show that a person's previous convictions may influence what symptoms they experience. In other words, specific beliefs, thoughts, and fears that a person held onto prior to the onset of schizophrenia can play a big role in forming thought patterns and delusions during the active stage of schizophrenia.

Chapter 3: Diagnosis and Treatment

The importance of seeking help directly following the onset of schizophrenia cannot be overstated. The earlier the intervention occurs, the more positive the outcomes of the treatment will be. In fact, proper treatment following a person's first psychotic episode decreases the occurrence of relapses by over 50%. Unfortunately, many people who experience the symptoms themselves may have their cognitive abilities affected to the point that they are not aware of their affects and therefore do not seek treatment for themselves. The longer schizophrenia goes untreated prior to participating in appropriate therapy and medicines, the less beneficial their effects.

There are a lot of difficulties that come with diagnosing schizophrenia. For the medical professional, this is due to the sporadic occurrence common to most schizophrenia manifestations, with many psychotic episodes coming and going unexpectedly. Not every patient of schizophrenia will experience an extremely severe psychotic episode that will lead to their hospitalization and subsequent diagnosis. For some, hallucinations begin so mildly that the person is not even sure if they experienced them. For those who suffer from delusions, however, they are likely to think that their beliefs are very real and that others simply do not understand them.

With the condition being so complex and dangerous, it becomes terrifyingly more life-threatening for those that do not receive adequate treatment. Numbers show that 69% of people suffering from schizophrenia lack the appropriate care that they require, with 90% of them living in countries of low- and middle-income levels. While the science and research behind schizophrenia continues to evolve, its treatments remain inaccessible to many. In the past, the aim was mainly to make the condition as easily manageable as possible. In other words, as long as the patient remained alive and their lack of extreme psychotic episodes made it easy for their caregivers to manage, the treatment was considered effective. Unfortunately, many countries who lack the funds to improve these standards continue employing the same techniques, taking away the potential of true recovery from many people with schizophrenia. In high-income countries, the focus of treatment for schizophrenia has thankfully shifted over the past couple of decades. Currently, treatments are being expanded to do more than just the bare minimum. There is still a long road ahead, as many people are still not using recovery as their true goal, but rather the management of symptoms throughout progressive deterioration. The inaccessibility to treatments in higher-income countries is almost always due to their costs.

Another factor that commonly endangers the wellbeing of patients with schizophrenia is misdiagnosis. Although schizophrenia is actually one of the most correctly diagnosed psychiatric disorders, with a 76.29% accuracy rate, it still leaves approximately a one in four chance for the person to initially get misdiagnosed. Due to some positive symptoms of schizophrenia increasing in severity over time, the initial symptoms of hyper and hypo activity can be mistaken for those of bipolar disorder. Bipolar disorder similarly involves symptoms of mood swings and time periods of high motivation and energy (mania) and those of a lack of activity (depression). The real danger of misdiagnosing psychiatric disorders stems from the subsequent treatment assigned to the patient. Although some of the treatment processes may be similar in name between many psychiatric disorders, the techniques used in psychotherapy, for example, can be very different and lead to undesirable results when used based on a misdiagnosed disorder. Unfortunately, black and Latino people suffering from schizophrenia are the ones most often misdiagnosed. Some believe the rate of misdiagnosis for people of these races is higher due to cultural misunderstandings.

Around the world, it has been found that rates of schizophrenia are almost double in countries of higher income. Evidently, this stems simply from their higher rates of diagnosis. Not only does this imply that there are many people around the globe living without a proper diagnosis and treatment, but it also means that the current statistic showing less than 1% of the world population being affected by schizophrenia is likely vastly underestimating the reality.

Medical Process of Diagnosing Schizophrenia

If you think you may have been experiencing signs of schizophrenia, begin by going to a primary care doctor or psychiatrist that will be able to perform a mental evaluation along with a physical exam. They will then proceed to ask about your family history of psychiatric disorders to help them identify any underlying risk factors that may increase your chances of developing schizophrenia. Due to some schizophrenic symptoms having similarities with those of some serious physical illnesses, medical professionals will often conduct some form of diagnostic tests, such as an MRI scan, CT scan, or even blood work to ensure that it is indeed a psychiatric disorder that is responsible for the experiences. Sometimes, a physical brain tumor may cause some similar effects. Oftentimes, even urine tests are employed to see if substance abuse may be causing the experiences. After physical causes are ruled out, the medical professional generally follows by referring you directly to a specialized psychiatrist. Psychiatrists are people who have completed at least 11 years of medical and psychological studies at the university level and are generally the senior clinicians in groups of psychologists. They are the ones who are generally in charge of coordinating a team of specialists and workers that will assist the individual through all areas of treatment for schizophrenia.

The process of diagnosing schizophrenia is difficult, long, and requires meticulous monitoring of symptoms. Just like many other psychiatric disorders, a diagnosis will be most accurate if the history of symptoms and how often they occur is taken into account. For schizophrenia, this can be a particularly lengthy process. In order for the medical professional to accurately diagnose the patient with schizophrenia, they must have experienced changes in their normal cognition and must present at least two of the positive symptoms of schizophrenia for a month-long time period. By tracking these symptoms for a long enough period of time, they decrease the chances of misdiagnosis. During the process of diagnosis, doctors and therapists always use diagnostic manuals to record and analyze symptoms described by the patient. In the past, these manuals included the DSM-4 and its predecessors, though these are often updated following any new discoveries. Currently, the standard is the Diagnostic and Statistical Manual of Mental Disorders (DSM-5), published by the American Psychiatric Association. It includes symptoms and steps to diagnose a total of approximately 157 different disorders. The DSM-5 is what is currently used to properly assess which mental illness the combined symptoms point to. Other techniques commonly used include a combination of the following:

- **Brief Psychiatric Rating Scale (BPRS).** A psychiatrist evaluates the severity of someone's schizophrenia through an approximately half-hour long conversation with the patient and their caregivers.

- **Cognitive tests.** These are used to assess one's capabilities with memory, thinking, language, and identification.

- **Personality tests.** These generally search for any personality traits common to those with schizophrenia, such as severe shyness, mistrust, doubt, lack of confidence, susceptibility to stress, and more.

- **Open-ended tests.** This is the continued search for similarities with signs of schizophrenia; a common test in this category is the Rorschach test.

These three types of tests are meant to assess the individual's cognitive abilities and observe if there are any abnormal thought processes that point to symptoms of schizophrenia.

General Treatment

As scary as this condition can seem, it is actually highly treatable. In fact, it is even more treatable than many physical illnesses, with the success rate for treatment being 60%. Again, it is important to remember that its success is heavily dependent on the timeframe during which treatment is sought out: the earlier, the better. The average amount of time that goes by between a person's first psychotic episode and receiving treatment is six to seven years. Within that time period, brain volume decreases, and relapses occur much more often than they would if the individual had already been receiving treatment. The following are the encouraged treatments for a person diagnosed with schizophrenia:

- Medication
- Psychotherapy
- Behavioral therapy

Psychiatric medication is required as soon as the patient is diagnosed. The antipsychotic medication is given to help the individual reduce and live through severe symptoms, such as hallucinations and delusions. There are two generations of antipsychotic medication, first generation—'typical'—and second generation—'atypical.' First generation antipsychotic medications are slightly older and are used primarily to tackle positive symptoms of schizophrenia. Unlike atypical antipsychotics, they decrease dopamine transmission. This category includes medications such as:

- Thorazine
- Prolixin
- Haldol
- Loxitane
- Trilafon
- Navane
- Stelazine

Second generation antipsychotic medications are a newer invention and include:

- Abilify
- Saphris
- Clozaril
- Fanapt
- Latuda
- Zyprexa
- Invega
- Risperdal
- Seroquel
- Geodon

Atypical antipsychotic medication is used generally to help stabilize negative symptoms, such as mood swings, decreases in motivation, and muddled thought processing. Among these, clozapine (clozaril) is one of a kind in antipsychotic medication, due to its unique ability to decrease suicidal thoughts in patients of schizophrenia. Unfortunately, even with the massive number of benefits provided by these medications, they can also cause some unwanted side effects. For the first category of medications—typical antipsychotics—these unwanted side effects commonly include movement problems along with muscle stiffness. Atypical antipsychotics, however, do not block dopamine; therefore, they commonly have different side effects. Rather than movement and muscle issues, atypical antipsychotics can cause weight gain and an increased chance of developing type two diabetes. Clozapine is arguably the most widely used antipsychotic for schizophrenia due to its 30% success rate in decreasing psychotic episodes in addition to the reduction of suicidal tendencies. Other side effects of both typical and atypical antipsychotic medications can include:

- Drowsiness
- Lightheadedness
- Dry mouth
- Nausea
- Low blood pressure
- Lower number of white blood cells

In addition to prescribed antipsychotics, psychotherapeutic treatments are also required for patients with schizophrenia. Psychotherapeutic treatments include individual therapy, group therapy, and cognitive behavioral therapy (CBT). The three types work together to both help the person understand and learn to manage their symptoms, as well as integrating into society in social situations. Individual therapy focuses on the former: The therapist teaches the person to deal with any intrusive thoughts and react in a way that does no further damage to them. Group therapy completes a similar task with the incorporation of other people who are in similar situations with a psychological disorder. Cognitive behavioral therapy (CBT) can help the person learn the triggers of their positive symptoms, such as hallucinations and delusions. Currently, the most effective drugs used to fight the positive symptoms of schizophrenia are not very useful for decreasing negative symptoms. This leaves many people with schizophrenia still less equipped in social situations. For this reason, when it is required, a psychiatrist may also encourage a fourth type of therapy, cognitive enhancement therapy (CET), that combines computer-based cognitive exercises and group therapy to improve the individual's social skills and cognitive functioning.

Once a person has been participating in treatment for some time, their psychiatrists implement the Positive and Negative Syndrome Scale (PANSS) in order to keep track of its effects. The PANSS test is generally done at common intervals and is similar to the BPRS test done during the initial diagnosis: The psychiatrist conducts a 30-minute interview and compares the results with previous ones to see how well the provided combination of medicine and therapy is working. They assess 30 different items outlined by the PANSS and provide a score between the range of 30 and 210 points. If they choose to conduct more detailed assessments, they are likely to turn to the Scale for the Assessment of Positive Symptoms (SAPS) and the Scale for the Assessment of Negative Symptoms (SANS) tests. The SANS looks at the patient for signs of any of the 25 total negative symptoms of schizophrenia while the SAPS does the same for 34 total positive symptoms. Over time, all of these results are compared to previous ones to indicate if treatment is working or if it should be altered to maximize its effectiveness. The good news is that, after 10 years following the diagnosis, approximately half of the people with schizophrenia are either recovered or treated enough to be able to live normally in society.

The cost of care, however, leaves many people either participating in only part of the treatments they need or without any treatment altogether. Schizophrenia is about two times more expensive to treat and recover from than depression. Many extreme costs are incurred if the patient has suicidal or violent tendencies that result in additional treatment, hospitalization, or arrest. The cost of properly treating schizophrenia can be as much as $57,000 in the United States a year. In the past, most of this annual cost came from hospital care; now, the majority of this cost is from antipsychotic medication due to an increase in its use. Unfortunately, due to its severity, schizophrenia increases people's poverty risk, and the only financial help some individuals with schizophrenia are able to receive is disability benefits, should they meet all requirements. People with severe positive symptoms of schizophrenia may choose to seek voluntary hospitalization if they feel like they are losing control over themselves or their symptoms. An average of 90,000 people across the United States are receiving care in a hospital for the condition at any given time. Once their symptoms are under control and are stable enough to return to their lives, they are released from the hospital. If the care requires more long-term treatment, some choose to be admitted to specialized psychiatric care centers. For the entire country of the United States, total costs accumulate to over $62 billion per year, of which $22.7 billion are direct costs and the rest are resulting from decreased productivity, homelessness, and other factors.

Self-Management Strategies

Professionals are required to prescribe medication, such as antipsychotics, and guide the patient through various therapy strategies and assessments. These official methods do wonders in terms of helping people with schizophrenia improve their lives and lead them as regularly as possible. However, each environment and situation is different for people with schizophrenia, and many look for additional ways to help themselves on their journey towards recovery. In fact, a study found that 48% of people living with schizophrenia heavily rely on techniques of self-management in order to manage their symptoms. Some common self-management strategies used by many people with schizophrenia are:

- Thinking of counter-arguments against their delusions
- Identifying some positive aspects of the condition, such as a feeling of connectedness to spirituality or nature and the ability to feel emotions stronger than the average person
- During times of deep mistrust in others, thinking back to any time periods in which they felt a strong love for someone

- Nurturing the positive relationships in their lives
- Reminding themselves of positive outcomes and cultivating optimism
- Creating an achievable routine and sticking to it as much as possible

Evidently, a lot of these self-management methods get easier with time and are strengthened by the essential therapy that one participates in. Together, therapy and self-management tricks make it easier for a person to break free from negative thought patterns and maximize their chances of recovery. Wonderfully, self-management eventually develops into a natural habit and continues to help the individual in minimizing the risk of relapse. In fact, 30% of people with schizophrenia live normally after 10 years of their diagnosis, even after stopping their use of antipsychotic medication.

Another helpful method in treating schizophrenia is the use of a support animal. Most commonly, people adopt a psychiatric assistance dog (PAD), or a service dog trained specifically for helping people diagnosed with a mental illness. They help the person by reducing anxiety and can even indicate whenever the person is showing signs of hallucination. However, some people resort to spending time around whatever other animal seems to decrease positive symptoms. For example, Molly Wilson, who was diagnosed with schizophrenia when she was just 16 years old, found that her auditory hallucinations faded when she spent time around horses. The connection and bond that can be formed between a person with schizophrenia and an animal can be a highly effective tool for self-management.

Chapter 4: History of Schizophrenia and Psychiatric Care

Schizophrenia and its complexities have posed a lot of trouble for people throughout its history, both to researchers trying to understand it as well as the patients who had to suffer from science's lack of knowledge on the subject. For the longest time, schizophrenia was not even identified as a separate condition, but rather treated the same as any other psychological disorder.

In the 12th century, the Bethlem—often called 'Bedlam'—was constructed as a means of providing a source of refuge for people who had trouble living in society. First, it was called the Priory of St. Mary of Bethlehem and was used in a religious sense. Later, it became known simply as the Bethlem hospital. For nearly five centuries, its priority was just to provide a place to stay for those that were too poor to afford their own housing. Eventually, people with mental illnesses started coming to the Bethlem due to their inability to care for themselves alone. It was reconstructed in the late 17th century and was officially declared to be an asylum. It was infamous for its magnificent exterior, even mirroring the looks of the Palace of Versailles in France, though its foundation was as weak and poorly constructed as the system of care it held within.

For centuries, the Bethlem was the only center of care in the United Kingdom available to those struggling with any and all mental illnesses. This, however, was not how it was defined, since mental illnesses were then regarded as physical illnesses and were treated as such. The treatments at Bethlem hospital therefore included induced vomiting, diarrhea, and bloodletting, all as means of purging the body of whatever it was that was making the person sick. These treatments were not stopped until the person was thought to be cured, obviously leading to most patients' deaths. The conditions inside were horrible and resembled more of a torturous jail than a place of refuge or care. Most doctors of that time believed that the mental illnesses experienced by the patients took away their sense of fear, shame, and regular emotions, making it 'acceptable' for them to be physically, verbally, and mentally abused by the staff. The chaotic and hellish environment of the Bethlem turned it into a huge tourist attraction and saw no improvement in care as job positions in the institution were given solely through nepotism. Bethlem offered no cures, treatments, or care, and posed a great risk of injury and death to those admitted. Regrettably, every following institution that was then built in an effort to provide a better place of care for those suffering from serious mental conditions such as schizophrenia met the same end as the conditions became more and more abusive.

Why, then, were so many people admitted to these so-called care centers? Usually, it was simply due to the discomfort and burden that people felt toward the affected individual's condition. All in all, these places were gruesome jails that prevented individuals with mental illness from affecting their friends and families.

Eventually, these disorders were recognized as something that had to do with the mind and not the physical body. These disorders were then categorized into the following four categories:

- Melancholia: similar to modern depression
- Mania: manic episodes
- Dementia: similar to modern schizophrenia
- Moral insanity: also similar to modern schizophrenia

Looking back now, it has been established that if a patient that was recorded to have melancholia, mania, and dementia at the same time, they were likely suffering from what is now known as bipolar disorder.

By the 19th century, more and more asylums were built in the United Kingdom, the United States, and many other countries. The conditions, however, were not much improved in many of the newer institutions. Baseless brain surgery, extreme electric shock therapy, and massive amounts of sedative drugs were used to 'treat' and contain the symptoms exhibited by patients. Many of these tactics remained well into the 20th century, with doctors at Willard Psychiatric Center in the United States administering a recorded 1443 shock treatments with no anesthesia or safeguards in the year 1943. The conditions of Willard saw no improvement over the next half of the century and it was finally closed for good in 1995. Throughout the 20th century, even asylums who did not employ such abusive methods for treatment were met with lots of criticism due to institutionalization; in other words, patients that managed to recover were not released due to their inability to re-assimilate themselves into society. This served as another reason for which major institutions for psychiatric care were being closed down and smaller, more local care centers were favored.

Current psychiatric care facilities do not resemble their predecessors. They are often smaller buildings, and do not lock away people with mental illnesses. Now, patients are given the privacy of their own room and are generally given an organized daily schedule that includes recreation, studies (if needed), group therapy, meals, and doctor visits. People often stay in such facilities anywhere from a couple days to several months and are generally able to leave at their own will if they were hospitalized voluntarily.

Early Beginnings

Before being misdiagnosed as a physical illness and then as a variety of mania, melancholia, dementia, or moral insanity, schizophrenia and similar psychological disorders were treated by religious figures. This was especially popular between the 14th and 16th centuries, during which it was believed that these conditions were caused by demonic possessions, pacts made with the devil, or a punishment for sins. Affected individuals during that time were often accused of witchcraft and burned at the stake, racking up a death count of tens of thousands of mentally ill people. In later centuries, exorcisms were a very common technique used to rid mentally ill people of the demons they were thought to be possessed by. Sometimes even the process of trepanation was used, which consisted of drilling holes in the skull of the affected person in an attempt to release the supernatural causes that were messing with their minds. Interestingly, it has been found that in the modern world, people with schizophrenia were likely to develop religiously themed delusions and hallucinations only after the fact that such a possibility was suggested to them.

Records of schizophrenia and similar psychological disorders date back to as early as 2000 BC. Texts describing symptoms similar to schizophrenia were found in ancient civilizations, ranging from the lands of modern-day African, Asian, and European countries. Many reflected the same convictions seen in the medieval era, of supernatural forces being responsible for the many conditions.

The person who is credited with identifying schizophrenia as a distinct psychological disorder was Dr. Emile Kraepelin in the late 19th century. He defined it as "a biological illness caused by anatomical or toxic processes". However, he referred to it as 'dementia praecox,' stemming from the previously accepted category of dementia used for diagnosing mental illnesses. He also believed that with age, dementia praecox would always evolve into full-blown dementia. The person who came to introduce the term schizophrenia and define it more closely to what it is today is the previously mentioned Swiss psychiatrist Eugen Bleuler in 1908. He is also the first person to truly recognize the variability of symptoms and claim that cognitive functioning of people with schizophrenia was not consistently altered but sometimes only in certain situations. He thought the unique factor in schizophrenia was the duality of both inhibited cognitive functioning, as well as a detachment from reality. This fundamental concept is what founded the identification of positive versus negative symptoms of schizophrenia.

Modern research is pointing to the likelihood of schizophrenia being contained in the same genes as those that provided humans' brains with their unique complexity. In fact, people became more likely to develop schizophrenia after homo sapiens evolved from Neanderthals. In other words, the more evolved humans became, the more susceptible they were to develop the condition. This indicates an interesting link between the gene that causes vulnerability to schizophrenia and those that increased humans' capabilities to survive. Otherwise, the gene's naturally fatal outcomes on the affected individual would have caused it to eventually disappear.

Past Misconceptions

Throughout history, schizophrenia has been misidentified as numerous things with a variety of supposed causes. These ideas cultivated a toxic culture surrounding this and all other mental illnesses that still has not been entirely dismantled.

The association of schizophrenia with religious and supernatural rationale caused many people to fear those affected. This is what consequently led to so many mentally ill people being killed for supposedly being witches. Others simply stayed away from those that were affected, and many families were much more willing to give up their loved one to a place like the Bethlem than to provide them with care themselves. They were often worried about getting possessed and attempted to protect themselves. Other than inciting fear in others, this association also brought further mental strain on the affected individual because of those saying their suffering from the condition was a punishment for their sins. Rather than being supported through their condition, they were shamed for these supposed sins and made to feel guilty for their condition, as though they had brought it upon themselves. Even in modern society, some people continue to deny the biological causes of schizophrenia and believe it is a divine being's will that causes a person to live with schizophrenia.

Beyond religion, the misunderstanding of schizophrenia has led to many people being labelled as simply lazy, attention-seeking, and irresponsible for being unable to live a regular life. In reality, laziness is a conscious act or choice of someone who is not affected by mental illness. With schizophrenia, it is avolition rather than laziness that causes the person's extreme lack of motivation, making it difficult for them to complete certain tasks. This is often considered one of the staple negative symptoms of schizophrenia and is present in other disorders as well, including depression and bipolar disorder. During psychotic episodes, it becomes even more excruciatingly difficult for a person to complete even the simplest of tasks, leaving them in a dangerous situation.

Due to these inaccurate accusations, many people with schizophrenia continue to be treated as outcasts and are even rejected by their friends and families. People closest to them hand them over to psychiatric care facilities and refuse to care for them. They are left without any form of a support system, become more likely to end up homeless and participate in substance abuse, and have severely limited resources as they begin their journey towards recovery in isolation.

The Process of Stigmatization

Although the history of stigmatization dates back to the first ever record of schizophrenic-like symptoms, there continues to be an abundance of societal systems that still push these notions. They blow schizophrenia out of proportion and, rather than take action towards making treatment accessible to more people, use it as nothing more than a captivating news story.

In fact, the media as a whole tends to relay information about schizophrenia through stories that only focus on the actions of the individual and not on how the mental illness has actually affected millions. This continues to allow people to blame those affected with the condition for actions that are often outside of their control. Furthermore, it examines schizophrenia through a lens that isolates each affected individual without ever looking at its mass effect. A lot of people have never been met with the realities of schizophrenia. Because of this, they rely on various forms of media to acquire information about it. The majority of entertainment and news outlets cause them to feel—either consciously or subconsciously—that people with schizophrenia should not be regarded as regular members of society. Chances are, most people who feel this way have actually come into contact with colleagues, friends, or acquaintances who live with psychological disorders, such as schizophrenia. The truth is that, unlike what some may think, individuals with such disorders are under no obligation to publicly disclose this information and can lead normal lives alongside those with no mental illnesses.

The lack of accessibility to treatments can often lead to homelessness and hospitalizations that repeat over and over again. In fact, a survey has found that approximately one in three homeless people in the United States suffer from schizophrenia and have no way to receive treatment. This is just one way that society criminalizes mental illness.

When a person who cannot afford treatment has a potentially dangerous psychotic episode, for example, they are not only arrested, but will likely be talked about in newspapers and on the news as yet another 'dangerous' person with schizophrenia, further stigmatizing everyone with the disorder. In fact, people with psychological disorders, such as schizophrenia and bipolar disorder, have a ten times higher chance of ending up in a jail cell than a hospital bed.

Chapter 5: Repercussions of Modern Stigmas

While things are improving, schizophrenia is still largely viewed as an inconvenience to the general public. The only difference is that now, in the 21st century, it would not work for society to lock people away in asylums with disgusting conditions. Instead, they do this a little more subtly, 'a little' being the keywords; anyone who spends just a little more time investigating the current treatment of people with schizophrenia will see just how deplorable the situation can be at times.

Society—largely the government—is failing people with psychological disorders. It seems to allocate so many funds to certain areas of society while completely neglecting others. With the way the government showcases where its priorities lie, it becomes quite clear just how far down the list people with mental illnesses are. In fact, they largely prefer the easy way out when it comes to this issue and choose to criminalize people with mental illnesses. Put simply, accusing and incarcerating people with mental illness is considerably cheaper than dedicating money towards treatment and rehabilitation resources for them. Furthermore, disorders such as schizophrenia require considerably more intensive—and therefore expensive—treatment than many of the more common mental illnesses, such as anxiety and depression. People with serious psychological disorders, such as schizophrenia, make up a much smaller part of society, making it easier for society to get away with their ostracization and mistreatment. Very few people who are not involved with schizophrenia in their lives are aware of the fact that nearly one in every three jails in the United States are holding people with serious psychological disorders with no charges, simply because they are waiting to be evaluated, or are waiting for a place in a psychiatric care center to open up. This is a very direct action that literally punishes people with mental illnesses and is hauntingly similar to the tactics used in medieval times.

People often defend these actions, saying that people with schizophrenia are often violent. However, that is a deep over-exaggeration. Only a small percentage of people with schizophrenia ever act violently towards others, comparable to the small percentage of the general public that becomes violent. In fact, people with schizophrenia are 14 times more likely to be victimized by an act of violence rather than be arrested for acting violently themselves. This is completely overlooked by the media, which does not show people the reality of the connection between violence and schizophrenia, where many people with the disorder are often targets of violence rather than perpetrators. This chance is only further increased by putting affected people into jails rather than treatment, where their vulnerability to violence is increased.

Jails are not the only societal systems in which people with schizophrenia are treated unfairly. The employment system and places of work completely lack accommodation for people suffering from a mental illness. People with schizophrenia are between six and seven times more likely to be out of a job than the general population. How, then, are they expected to pay for the necessary treatments that would allow them to live life normally? The answer simply does not bother those that are not affected by schizophrenia. This unacceptably normalized phenomenon will only begin to change when measures are put into place that will adjust the employment system to allow people with schizophrenia to find and hold work.

Another common misconception about schizophrenia is that it is caused by bad parenting. This belief first gained popularity after the introduction of Sigmund Freud's psychoanalytical theories. While there is clear evidence linking childhood trauma with the onset of the disorder, a child raised in a non-abusive environment is not going to develop schizophrenia solely because their parents made a few parenting mistakes.

This is not the only misconception about schizophrenia that puts the spotlight of shame onto parents. People often expect those with schizophrenia to be incapable of leading normal lives. This is reflected by the idea that people with schizophrenia should not take it upon themselves to start a family or bring up children. This is not just because they fear the slightly increased chance for their offspring to develop the condition, too; they also assume that these people are unfit for such a task. If treatment is participated in accordingly, people with schizophrenia can be completely capable of being good and stable parents. In fact, a study found that 70% of people with parents who have schizophrenia were happy with the parenting they received from them. Raising a child is much more about the dedication to being a good parent; both for people with schizophrenia and those without. If a parent experiences occasional episodes of psychosis, it is often a good idea to explain this to their children in a way that is appropriate to their age. This way, their child is aware of what to expect and accepts it as just something that happens rather than being scared by their perception of it.

Parents should be well aware of the warning signs of schizophrenia in order to know what to look for if their child is showing any symptoms. It is because people think schizophrenia occurs so rarely and assume a child may be just acting lazy or immature that seeking treatment is often delayed. By knowing the signs, parents are more likely to start treatment earlier if necessary and maximize their child's chances at growing up into well-adjusted adults. Although the diagnosis rarely happens at a young age, the mistreatment of school-aged children with schizophrenia is not uncommon. Due to both positive and negative symptoms of the condition, many children are unable to go to public or private school, at least for the duration of particularly difficult psychotic episodes. Often, parents of kids with schizophrenia opt for home-schooling. Although this alternative has its own benefits, it may increase the child's isolation and prevent them from building useful social skills for their future. Those children that do continue to go to public schools are often the victims of bullying, which may turn them against social interaction altogether. Furthermore, the way that information is taught in a classroom setting may not always be the best way for children with schizophrenia to absorb and remember, effectively slowing their progress down.

Destigmatizing Schizophrenia

The process of destigmatizing schizophrenia begins with each individual person. Those that are not aware of its harmful effects will not be inclined towards stopping or calling out misrepresentation, stereotypes, and limits put on people with schizophrenia. The burden of changing normalized misconceptions should not be once again put on those living with the condition, but rather the general population that currently plays an active role in perpetuating them. It is up to people without schizophrenia to work together to create a more accepting environment.

This begins with perhaps the most important and all-encompassing act of education. When people think about education, their minds often go directly towards formal education, such as grade school, colleges, and universities. In reality, education comes to us in all forms of media and what we interact with in our surrounding environment. While we are still far away from being able to incorporate adequate material about mental illnesses into the school system, it is up to us to help educate those around us. Even for parents without schizophrenia, talking to their children about the importance of mental health takes away the power for it to be stigmatized in their minds. They learn that people live with various illnesses— even ones that they cannot physically see—and will respect these differences. The change we want to see in systems, such as places of work and the faulty methods of incarceration, begins with people who are taught to value others whether or not their physical and mental abilities and health are the same as their own. Of course, with the education about mental illnesses currently in use, it comes as no surprise that children are turning into adults afraid of the wrong thing: the people with the mental illness instead of the unfair treatment they endure. Rather than relying on the one or two infamous movies that provide poor representation of people with schizophrenia, people involved in entertainment should push for more media that stops showing the condition from a singular point of view and provides accurate examples of its spectrum.

It may sound tedious to complete, but it is through this step-by-step approach of educating each individual that change on a larger scale can be finally made. Eventually, there will be an increasing number of people who push for policy change and allocate government funds more appropriately, making treatment more and more accessible. Rehabilitation will finally become the priority, and the past system of criminalization and blame will become a distant memory. Things are slowly changing and improving, and we have undoubtedly come a long way, but there is still much more to be done on this front.

Changing the Narrative and Coping with Stigma

Currently, some people are advocating for schizophrenia to be reclassified altogether as a brain disease like Alzheimer's. The aim of this proposition is to eliminate the extreme amount of stigma surrounding schizophrenia and to perhaps move more money into research about it in order to discover more treatment options. This is because of the sad reality that mental illnesses are not treated as seriously as physical illnesses. The organization, called Schizophrenia and Related Disorders Alliance of America, is encouraging Congress to include schizophrenia in a CDC program that will allow for more research to be conducted on underlying neurological factors. This, in turn, will spark research into not only additional treatments, but even a possible cure of schizophrenia. People with neurological diseases are considerably less likely to be blamed for their conditions and more likely to receive proper care than people with psychological disorders. Through this new definition of schizophrenia, other psychological disorders, such as bipolar disorder, may be the next to be examined.

An inspiring youth activist, Amanda Southworth, is also making a big step towards normalizing the acceptance of mental illnesses. She is currently looking to create an app that will help people with schizophrenia identify when they are experiencing hallucinations. Objectively, she is doing more work towards de-stigmatizing psychological disorders than entire communities of adults. It is unfortunate that big companies in Silicon Valley may never prioritize the creation of such apps simply because they are considered to be less financially profitable, but people like Amanda Southworth are proof that the future for mentally ill people is much brighter than the past.

For people living with schizophrenia, stigma is one of the leading outside factors that contribute to emotional turmoil. It can cause guilt, increased social anxiety, and a preference to hide the reality of their struggles out of fear of being judged and shunned. Coping with stigma is a whole other burden put onto those affected by the condition. Those who struggle with its effects can even avoid getting the treatment they require out of fear of the injustice they might face as someone labelled as mentally ill. Some steps to consider for those dealing with this stigma include:

- Rid yourself of internalized shame influenced by society's wrongful perception of schizophrenia.

- Do not let your illness define you; schizophrenia is not all that you are and does not dictate who you are or can be.

- Do not let others convince you of what you are and are not capable of.

- Join a support group to engage in a safe environment and see that you are not alone in your journey.

- Be honest with medical professionals to ensure you are receiving the most appropriate treatment.

- Find supportive people and actively socialize with them.

Chapter 6: Supporting a Loved One with Schizophrenia

Perhaps the scariest part of schizophrenia is its ability to pass under the radar for years. It does not make itself obvious while it slowly makes its way into someone's cognitive functions, socializing abilities, and perception of reality. It can spend years fooling people, making them aware something about them is off but not alarming them to the point of seeking help. Sometimes, before it can be contained, it finally makes itself known through a first ever episode of psychosis. The individual risks becoming their own worst enemy during a time like that.

For someone on the outside, watching a loved one go through such a traumatic experience is extremely difficult. You can be faced with guilt, blaming yourself for not having noticed it sooner, or feeling ashamed that you were not able to help calm their episode of psychosis. The truth is that thinking this way and everything that comes with it is counterproductive. When schizophrenia has never been encountered before, most people don't know what the warning signs are. However, even knowing these signs may not always help. It can be extremely difficult encouraging a person you fear has schizophrenia to seek treatment. In a situation where a loved one refuses to get treatment, the best you can do is provide them with enough support that eventually may incline them to listen to your suggestions. Forcing a person to seek help against their will can not only cause them to reject the idea even more strongly but can create a hostile environment in which they feel like they are being rejected.

It is no doubt that watching a loved one suffer from something that could very much be treated is difficult and heart-wrenching. However, it is not only your point of view to consider. Their reality, their experiences, and their struggles have their own validity and deserve to be recognized. In a situation where treatment or the idea of seeking help is rejected, the most positive effect will come from your unconditional support. You may not have to agree or encourage their decisions but showing that you are there for them will go an incredibly long way.

For a person with schizophrenia, perceptions as we know them are altered, causing them to feel incredibly isolated. Once again, with your care and support, the threats they think are facing them may melt away. Validate their experiences. Dedicate a piece of your time to carefully listen to whatever they may have to say. To truly help them, you must do your best to understand what they are going through.

As any person who has a loved one living with schizophrenia, you wish for them to get better. This is a journey that involves both of you, and its adversities rope you in with them. To offer the best support you can and further de-stigmatize schizophrenia, talk about your own mental health openly. This also serves as an effective method of taking the spotlight of mental illness off of your loved one. It shows that mental struggles affect not only them and can create a stronger bond between the two of you.

Living With Schizophrenia

Along with professional treatments, many people are encouraged to lead lifestyles that offer them stability. Minimizing the occurrence of shocking or life-changing events helps prevent unnecessary emotional distress, in turn making the road to easing symptoms of schizophrenia significantly smoother. Unfortunately, this leaves many people with schizophrenia at a disadvantage when it comes to pursuing romantic relationships. Even non-romantic relationships are often put under strain, with many family members and friends of the affected individual not wanting to take responsibility for their care. Not only is this harmful to their emotional wellbeing, without adequate support, this puts them at a higher risk of being mistreated and overlooked in the medical system.

Approximately, a mere 20% of people diagnosed with schizophrenia are able to hold a job in the primary labor market. Depending on their level of financial stability, unemployment can strike, and money may quickly become a problem. Depending on the severity of their symptoms and financial problems, homelessness and poor living conditions are not far away. If your loved one is facing such a situation, evaluate whether you are in a place in your life from which you could help accommodate them. The good news is, with proper medication, your loved one has significantly higher chances of providing for themselves once things improve. You could start by making a list of expenses and budget out how much you are able to provide them with. However, if giving money is not possible in your situation, consider helping them apply for government benefits or even organize a fundraiser on their behalf.

Many people watching a loved one live with schizophrenia are most shocked by the first episode of psychosis that they may witness. Their primary fear is that they will cause damage to themselves. In a situation as time sensitive as this one, people who have never dealt with such an event are at a loss for how to act. In situations that escalate to potentially dangerous ones, many people do not know whether or not to call 911 for help. If the answer is affirmative to any of the following questions, calling 911 may be the best choice to ensure everyone's safety:

- Are they threatening to cause any harm to themselves or anyone else?
- Do they have any history of past suicide attempts?
- Are they not capable of feeding or dressing themselves?
- Do they live on the street?

If an episode of psychosis is less threatening, the steps are to remain calm, listen, and react according to your loved one's actions. Depending on their experiences, your presence may actually appear to them as a threat due to certain hallucinations or delusions; this should never be taken personally. The best way to communicate at this time is in short and clear sentences that cannot be misinterpreted and are more easily perceived. Stay away from providing any positive or negative feedback, no matter how bizarre anything they say may sound to you.

All of this can prove to be a lot of mental strain on a caregiver to someone with schizophrenia. Setting up your own support system is a healthy and effective way of making sure that you are not letting your own mental health decline. Even without the presence of a mental illness, a good therapist could help ease any distress experienced from caregiving.

With both positive and negative symptoms, schizophrenia makes keeping up with relationships incredibly hard. Studies have found that approximately 70% of people with schizophrenia are unable to maintain a strong relationship. The lump of this majority is mostly people who are not receiving proper care. With the right treatments, a stable relationship is considerably more doable. Dating with schizophrenia relies on this even more, since even the healthiest of romantic relationships can face strain if episodes of psychosis repeat frequently and are hard to manage. All partnerships require sacrifices, understanding, and mutual support, but especially ones where schizophrenia is involved. Due to potentially more complicated trust issues, a romantic relationship like this requires a very strong bond. Provide them with reassurance whenever they communicate any of their doubts. If someone is dating a person with schizophrenia, rather than thinking their partner will be completely dependent on them, they must be dedicated to what every other adult relationship is founded on: open communication and treating each other with respect.

Importance of a Supportive Environment

The stigma that makes it seem as though people with schizophrenia are simply not meant for maintaining relationships could potentially cause them to self-stereotype, consequently convincing themselves that it is true. With this mindset, the person will continue to completely lack any motivation to even attempt increasing their social interaction. Someone who has been convinced they will fail will simply never try.

However, this keeps them from using something that could play a key role in their improvement. In fact, studies show that stable relationships with others can not only improve symptoms, but can even decrease the chances of future episodes of psychosis and quicken their overall recovery. The power of these social ties is nearly as important as antipsychotic medications and therapy.

A person with schizophrenia could potentially become so comfortable with their professional therapist that they believe additional relationships will not offer anything critical to them. Although a high level of trust and honesty is required between a patient and their therapist, having deep relationships—such as healthy ties with family, friendships, and romantic partners—provides a completely different type of support.

Conclusion

Life throws curve balls when we least expect them. Sometimes, the chances of something happening—good or bad—are as small as ever, yet that is precisely what happens to you. A majority of people do not assume that they or a loved one will experience schizophrenia, leaving them not knowing what to expect when someone does happen to develop it. However, with the right resources, the risk of schizophrenia becomes less and less threatening, not because it diminishes, but because they feel more capable of handling anything that it may involve. This allows them to embark on their journey to recovery, not with fear, but with acceptance and determination. A person who has taken time to understand schizophrenia for the sake of someone else in their life can be providing exactly what they may need the most: another person who is determined for them to recover.

While the world continues to revolve around trivial stereotypes about schizophrenia, stick to prioritizing the well-being of yourself and of those you love. The signs of schizophrenia you have learned about could possibly make the difference between a loved one ending up living on the streets and overcoming their symptoms and taking care of themselves just like anyone else. Prescribed antipsychotics and therapy provide the solid foundation to a flourishing future filled with rehabilitation, self-sufficiency, and happiness. The loving understanding you provide them with could have a significant impact that you are not even aware of.

Schizophrenia impacts every corner of someone's life: how they think, how they feel, what they see, etc. It goes beyond tendencies towards self-isolation or a lack of motivation; it can create a world—or rather, a void—that has the person fighting against themselves and their hallucinations or delusions. However, the difficulty and threat that schizophrenia poses does not only stem from itself. A large part of why people fear it so much is simply the way it is portrayed and the additional adversity of society making it difficult to access treatments. This way, schizophrenia not only varies in its symptoms, but also the outcome one can expect from it. Will they end up homeless? Can they even afford all the treatments they require? What if they end up in jail, locked up for actions that they barely had any control over?

Society continues to stand on what their ancestors have built—a faulty foundation of discrimination that still has a hold on our collective understanding of mental illness. It seems to crave criminalizing those who struggle with their mental health in order to preserve whatever needs or wants the rest of the population has. Slowly, the advocates of the world fighting for mental health—people just like you who have taken the step towards educating themselves—are helping it stop revolving around the comfort and desires of only part of their population while the rest are being treated like their value to society is replaceable. In fact, every person who takes the step in reevaluating their own behaviors and mindsets in regards to schizophrenia and similar psychological disorders is playing a part in making that happen.

Whether schizophrenia has influenced your life or not, change starts with you and stops at whoever your positive actions end up reaching. Taking the time to read this book and educate yourself on schizophrenia was a commendable step, and I thank you for taking it.

References

Ayano, G., Demelash, S., yohannes, Z., Haile, K., Tulu, M., Assefa, D., Tesfaye, A., Haile, K., Solomon, M., Chaka, A., & Tsegay, L. (2021). Misdiagnosis, detection rate, and associated factors of severe psychiatric disorders in specialized psychiatry centers in Ethiopia. *Annals of General Psychiatry*, *20*(1). https://doi.org/10.1186/s12991-021-00333-7

Bar, K.-J., & Ebert, A. (2010). Emil Kraepelin: A pioneer of scientific understanding of psychiatry and psychopharmacology. *Indian Journal of Psychiatry*, *52*(2), 191. https://doi.org/10.4103/0019-5545.64591

Barse, M. (2017, July 23). *Some schizophrenia patients can cope without medication.* Sciencenordic.com. https://sciencenordic.com/denmark-psychology-videnskabdk/some-schizophrenia-patients-can-cope-without-medication/1447561

Bhugra, D. (2005). The Global Prevalence of Schizophrenia. *PLoS Medicine*, *2*(5), e151. https://doi.org/10.1371/journal.pmed.0020151

Booth, S. (2020). *What Is Schizophrenia Prodrome?* WebMD. https://www.webmd.com/schizophrenia/schizophrenia-prodrome

Casarella, J. (Ed.). (2021). *What's the Prognosis for Someone With Schizophrenia?* WebMD; WebMD. https://www.webmd.com/schizophrenia/schizophrenia-outlook

Centre for Addiction and Mental Health. (2020, June 18). *Suicide rate for people with schizophrenia spectrum disorders over 20 times higher than the general population.* CAMH. https://www.camh.ca//en/camh-news-and-stories/suicide-rate-for-people-with-schizophrenia-spectrum-disorders

Fleischhacker, W. W., Arango, C., Arteel, P., Barnes, T. R. E., Carpenter, W., Duckworth, K., Galderisi, S., Halpern, L., Knapp, M., Marder, S. R., Moller, M., Sartorius, N., & Woodruff, P. (2014). Schizophrenia--Time to Commit to Policy Change. *Schizophrenia Bulletin, 40*(Suppl 3), S165–S194. https://doi.org/10.1093/schbul/sbu006

Gogos, A., Sbisa, A. M., Sun, J., Gibbons, A., Udawela, M., & Dean, B. (2015). A Role for Estrogen in Schizophrenia: Clinical and Preclinical Findings. *International Journal of Endocrinology, 2015,* 1–16. https://doi.org/10.1155/2015/615356

Greenstein, L. (2017). *Can Stigma Prevent Employment? | NAMI: National Alliance on Mental Illness.* Nami.org.

https://www.nami.org/Blogs/NAMI-Blog/October-2017/Can-Stigma-Prevent-Employment

Grover, S., Davuluri, T., & Chakrabarti, S. (2014). Religion, spirituality, and schizophrenia: A review. *Indian Journal of Psychological Medicine*, *36*(2), 119. https://doi.org/10.4103/0253-7176.130962

Hardy, J. (2015, January 29). *Divine Madness: a History of Schizophrenia*. History Cooperative; The History Cooperative. https://historycooperative.org/divine-madness-a-history-of-schizophrenia/

Hemphill, R. E. (1966). Historical Witchcraft and Psychiatric Illness in Western Europe. *Proceedings of the Royal Society of Medicine*, *59*(9), 891–902. https://doi.org/10.1177/003591576605900947

Herbert, H. S., Manjula, M., & Philip, M. (2013). Growing Up with a Parent having Schizophrenia: Experiences and Resilience in the Offsprings. *Indian Journal of Psychological Medicine*, *35*(2), 148–153. https://doi.org/10.4103/0253-7176.116243

Holland, K. (2019, November 26). *Understanding the Phases of Schizophrenia*. Healthline; Healthline Media. https://www.healthline.com/health/mental-health/phases-of-schizophrenia

Howard, R. (Director). (2001). *A Beautiful Mind* [Film]. Universal Pictures.

Kapil, R. (2019, February 6). *5 Surprising Mental Health Statistics.* Mental Health First Aid. https://www.mentalhealthfirstaid.org/2019/02/5-surprising-mental-health-statistics/

Levine, H. (2021, January 26). *Support Animals for Schizophrenia.* WebMD. https://www.webmd.com/schizophrenia/features/emotional-support-animals-schizophrenia

Lumen. (2008). *Mental Health Treatment: Then and Now | Introduction to Psychology.* Lumenlearning.com. https://courses.lumenlearning.com/wmopen-psychology/chapter/introduction-to-mental-health/

Mental Help. (2015a). *Evidence That Schizophrenia is a Brain Disease.* Mentalhelp.net; https://www.mentalhelp.net/schizophrenia/evidence-its-a-brain-disease/

Mental Help. (2015b). *Schizophrenia Symptoms, Patterns and Statistics and Patterns.* Mentalhelp.net; https://www.mentalhelp.net/schizophrenia/statistics/

Mental Illness Policy Org. (2019). *Homeless Mentally Ill Facts and Figures - Mental Illness Policy Org.* Mental Illness

Policy   Org. https://mentalillnesspolicy.org/consequences/homeless-mentally-ill.html

Miller, C. (n.d.). *First Psychotic Episode: Why Early Treatment is Critical.* Child Mind Institute. https://childmind.org/article/first-episode-psychosis-early-treatment-critical/

National Alliance on Mental Illness. (2018). *Facts On Schizophrenia | NAMI: National Alliance on Mental Illness.* Nami.org. https://www.nami.org/Press-Media/Press-Releases/1998/Facts-On-Schizophrenia

National Alliance on Mental Illness. (2020a). *Schizoaffective Disorder | NAMI: National Alliance on Mental Illness.* Nami.org. https://www.nami.org/About-Mental-Illness/Mental-Health-Conditions/Schizoaffective-Disorder

Ohwovoriole, T. (2021, February 5). *What Role Does Genetics Play In Causing Schizophrenia?* Verywell Mind. https://www.verywellmind.com/link-between-schizophrenia-and-genetics-5094107

Patel, K. R., Cherian, J., Gohil, K., & Atkinson, D. (2014). Schizophrenia: Overview and Treatment Options. *P & T : A Peer-Reviewed Journal for Formulary Management, 39*(9), 638–645.

Physical Health and Schizophrenia. (n.d.). Living with Schizophrenia. https://livingwithschizophreniauk.org/information-sheets/physical-health-schizophrenia/

Popovic, D., Schmitt, A., Kaurani, L., Senner, F., Papiol, S., Malchow, B., Fischer, A., Schulze, T. G., Koutsouleris, N., & Falkai, P. (2019). Childhood Trauma in Schizophrenia: Current Findings and Research Perspectives. *Frontiers in Neuroscience,* *13*(274). https://doi.org/10.3389/fnins.2019.00274

Rokita, K. I., Holleran, L., Dauvermann, M. R., Mothersill, D., Holland, J., Costello, L., Kane, R., McKernan, D., Morris, D. W., Kelly, J. P., Corvin, A., Hallahan, B., McDonald, C., & Donohoe, G. (2020). Childhood trauma, brain structure and emotion recognition in patients with schizophrenia and healthy participants. *Social Cognitive & Affective Neuroscience,* *15*(12), 1336–1350. https://doi.org/10.1093/scan/nsaa160

Ruiz, R. (2018, May 27). *8 inspiring, youth mental health activists you need to follow.* Mashable. https://mashable.com/article/inspiring-youth-mental-health-activists-to-follow

Schizophrenia Facts and Statistics. (2013). Schizophrenia.com. http://schizophrenia.com/szfacts.htm#

Smith, K. (2016). *Schizophrenia & Depression - Understanding The Link & Potential Risk.* PsyCom.net. https://www.psycom.net/schizophrenia-and-depression

Storvestre, G. B., Jensen, A., Bjerke, E., Tesli, N., Rosaeg, C., Friestad, C., Andreassen, O. A., Melle, I., & Haukvik, U. K. (2020, May 5). *Childhood Trauma in Persons With Schizophrenia and a History of Interpersonal Violence.* Frontiers; Frontiers Psychiatry. https://www.frontiersin.org/articles/10.3389/fpsyt.2020.00383/full

Treatment Advocacy Center. (2008). *Schizophrenia – Fact Sheet.* Treatment Advocacy Center. https://www.treatmentadvocacycenter.org/evidence-and-research/learn-more-about/25-schizophrenia-fact-sheet

Treatment Advocacy Center. (2017). *Criminalization of Mental Illness.* Treatment Advocacy Center. https://www.treatmentadvocacycenter.org/key-issues/criminalization-of-mental-illness

University of Liverpool. (2012). *Childhood trauma linked to schizophrenia.* ScienceDaily. https://www.sciencedaily.com/releases/2012/04/120419102440.htm

Wilson, L. S., Gitlin, M., & Lightwood, J. (2011, April 5). *Schizophrenia Costs for Newly Diagnosed Versus Previously Diagnosed Patients*. Pharmacy Times. https://www.pharmacytimes.com/view/ajpb_11marapr _wilson_107to115

World Health Organisation. (2019, April 9). *Schizophrenia*. Who.int; World Health Organization: WHO. https://www.who.int/news-room/fact-sheets/detail/schizophrenia

Zhu, B., Ascher-Svanum, H., Faries, D. E., Peng, X., Salkever, D., & Slade, E. P. (2008). Costs of treating patients with schizophrenia who have illness-related crisis events. *BMC Psychiatry*, *8*(1). https://doi.org/10.1186/1471-244x-8-72